MESSAGE TO MY NEIGHBOR

JEFFERY ADAMSON

ISBN 978-1-7782268-0-9

Mikel and Alec my faithful coworkers
– thank you for all your help sharing these messages
to our neighbours and now to our world.

My mom, Ivy. Thank you, your support
means the world to me.

Contents

SIN

INTRODUCTION OF SIN

The new "normal" is here. The wearing of masks, to cover mouth and noses, for entry into all stores. There is a new language with now well-defined terms such as "social distancing" and "self-isolation." COVID-19 self-assessments, assessment centers, and the wait for a cure are all part of the new normal. The fear of catching this virus is real, and while some might not have caught COVID-19, all are feeling its impact.

This is equivalent to what happened in the Garden of Eden – the paradise that Adam and Eve once occupied. This paradise was lost due to the virus of sin. Prior to sin there was no need for bodily covering. There was a direct connection between man and God, there was no separation, no social distance, no self-isolation. However, after sin entered the world, clothes of skin were sewn to cover their nakedness. There remained a wait for a cure, a promised deliverer who would remedy the world from the effects of the virus of sin. Even today we continue to hide and run away from God. New terms have been added to our lexicon such as "justification," "sanctification," and "salvation."

This is our normal. We are so accustomed to living in a world with sin that we can hardly imagine a world without it. A world without death; a world without evil, a world where thoughts and actions are pure, a world where bodily coverings are unnecessary. A world where communication with God does not require a mediator. A world where living in God's presence is not a fearful idea.

While we adjust to a world with COVID-19, remember that everything that ails this world is the consequence of sin. COVID-19 is a symptom of the virus of sin.

Our only hope is in the person of Jesus, the promised Messiah. The Lamb of God who takes away the sins of this world. This same Jesus who died for our sins, so that we may live again. The mediator between God and man. Jesus who pours out his Holy Spirit to seal his believers so they may inherit the earth when it is made new.

Let us not fear sin or COVID-19, but let us trust in the Lord Jesus, the son of God. Perfect love removes all fear and Jesus' love for us is perfect. He destroyed the power of sin on the cross and by this action displayed his love for the world.

If you are fearful of COVID-19, worried about the new normal, do not be discouraged. There is nothing new under the sun. This act has already happened, and the remedy is here!

Will you accept Jesus as the remedy for the virus of sin? Jesus, the Great Physician who heals and raises the dead, wants to heal us from sin. He has the power to heal us from COVID-19 and many other sicknesses, all caused by sin. If we believe and accept him at his Word, and what he has done for us, we will enter paradise. Then we will experience the joy of his creation as he intended.

FAITH

BELIEVE ON THE LORD JESUS CHRIST

It has been two months of self-isolation. With each day bringing new concerns. Many people are perplexed as to what is happening in the world. Do not fear! The Bible advises that these things must happen. But what are we to do? What must I do to be saved?

The answer is found in Acts 16:25–31. In this story, a jailer, who is in charge of his prisoners finds them all free. Afraid, he reaches for his sword to kill himself out of fear, supposing that the prisoners have fled. However, the prisoners call to him, and say, "Don't do it – we are all here."

In our age, what is imprisoned, is the TRUTH. But what is truth? "Jesus answered, 'I am the way and the truth and the life. No one comes to the Father except through me'" (John 14:6).

Unfortunately, many, out of fear, do not accept the TRUTH. Fear of being ostracized, fear from being ashamed for their beliefs. However, they will lose their lives by believing the lie.

In our present situation where the *foundation of our society is crumbling before our eyes,* people have nothing to hold on to, just like the jailer, and many are ready to take their own life. Many are suffering from mental health issues due to the trauma of their life. Many are suffering in silence, and medicating their problems with drugs, alcohol, or some other vice to hide their true condition of hopelessness.

This was the situation in which the jailer found himself, as he was about to take his own life. He failed at his job, and did not want to face the potential consequences – so he was ready to give up on life. However, hope came from the unlikeliest source: the prisoners. Who encouraged him not to take his own life!

Then they brought in a light, and he could see and came out of the jail. His first question was, "What must I do to be saved?"

The answer given, then, is the same answer now: *Believe on the Lord Jesus Christ, and you will be saved, you and your household.* The jailer believed, studied the Word of God, and he and his household were baptized that very night.

And another amazing part of the story is that the jailer – rejoicing and believing in God with all his house – and the prisoners sit and eat together. This rejoicing may not happen for all on earth, but is promised for all in heaven.

Jesus' Competed Work

Have you ever received an offer so good, you would be foolish to refuse it? I want to share with you such an offer. Esau, the first-born son of Isaac, was in line to receive the blessings promised to Abraham. This was his by right as the first-born son. Nonetheless, he gave it up. Jesus as the only begotten Son of God was the inheritor of eternal life. Nonetheless, he gave it up. Both men freely gave up what was theirs by right. Will you accept what is being offered to you?

To receive this blessing requires a few things. First, we must accept the terms of the exchange. Second, it requires sacrifice. Third, it requires a remarkable change in our person. Then finally, we approach the Father and present ourselves for judgment. If we make it through the judgment, then we will receive the blessing and its resulting inheritance.

Jacob, while Esau was at death's door, said, "Give me your birthright."

Esau offered it to Jacob and an exchange took place (Genesis 25:33). Now when Isaac was old and dying, he wanted to bless his firstborn son. Jacob with the help of his mother, Rebekah, sacrificed two kids of the goats and prepared a savory meal for his Father. Rebekah dressed Jacob in Esau's finest clothing (Genesis 27:15) and covered his exposed skin with the goatskins. Isaac ate the meal, and then drank the wine. He felt his son and smelt his body and was unable to discern that it was Jacob and not Esau. As a result, Isaac blessed Jacob, who then became the recipient of the blessing (Genesis 27:30). Esau later came to the Father and was rejected. Even though he sought the blessing with tears, there was none available to him (Genesis 27:33).

Like Jacob, when Jesus was at death's door, he gave up his birthright – eternal life. Anyone willing to accept this exchange by faith, to them it belongs (Ephesians 2:8–9; 1 Peter 1:3–5). This exchange is a life for life, and is obtained only by sacrifice. The savory soup could be prepared only by the death of two kids of the goats. Likewise, the garments of Christ must be worn (Ephesians 6:13–17; Colossians 3:5–14; Revelation 19:8). Our lives, our bodies, our characters must be so changed that when we approach the judgment seat of God no distinction can be made between Jesus and ourselves (2 Corinthians 5:10). This is the only way to obtain eternal life. Christ sought it with tears (Luke 22:42–44), but was rejected (Matthew 27:46) and afflicted to present this offer to us (Isaiah 53:3–5).

Will you reject such a great offer? Our inheritance is death

(Hebrews 9:27); Jesus' inheritance is eternal life. Will you make the exchange?

> For if the word spoken through angels proved steadfast, and every transgression and disobedience received a just reward how shall we escape if we neglect so great a salvation, which at the first began to be spoken by the Lord, and was confirmed to us by those who heard Him, God also bearing witness both with signs and wonders, with various miracles, and gifts of the Holy Spirit, according to His own will? (Hebrews 2:2–4)

Jacob had to meet Esau, and we will one day have to meet Jesus. That meeting will result in eternal damnation or eternal life.

Will you refuse this offer?

SAMSON AND THE JUDGMENT

Do you remember the story of Samson the Nazarite, who from birth was endowed with supernatural strength? Samson's strength was given to him for the purpose of delivering Israel from the oppression of the Philistines (Judges 13:5). His responsibility was to maintain his strength by refraining from having his hair cut.

Samson abused his power and broke his vows. His behavior was wretched: he was given over to sexual immortality and lay with a prostitute (Judges 16:1). This was supposed to be a man of God, who was set apart from birth. However, he was compromised. He poured all his heart into a woman who was seeking to have him destroyed for the love of money (Judges 16:17). As a result of going astray, he found himself blind and in bondage.

Samson has many similarities to the church of today (Revelation 3:15–17). The church has compromised many of its core beliefs. The church has not respected its head, Jesus Christ, and has severed its connection to him. Many are given over to sexual impurity with women. A gaze on the news shows a litany of people proclaiming to be Christians, yet caught in many scandals. The church, the people of God, are powerless and blind. They are unaware of their condition (Revelation 3:17) and cannot discern, until crises arise, that God has departed from them.

This was the story of Samson! He gave away the secret to his strength and his seven locks were severed. He awoke expecting, as always, to defeat the Philistines. On this occasion, he lacked strength, for the spirit of God had departed. The Philistines bound him and gouged out his eyes. Likewise, our culture is imploding: morality has hit a nadir. The church is enfeebled and unable to mount a resistance, for it is blind.

Fortunately for Samson, he recognized his failure. He cried out to God, asking the Lord "to remember and strengthen" him that he might avenge his enemies for taking his sight (Judges 16:28). The Lord heard his prayer and strengthened Samson. Samson then pushed hard against the two pillars and the temple fell upon the Philistines. In this effort, resulting in his death, Samson killed many of the Philistines.

Today, we need a people to cry out to God, saying, "Remember me; give me strength to avenge the evils of our day." If we push hard against the two pillars of "love for God and love for man," then the world's institutions and precepts not built upon the sure foundation of God's Word will fall.

Jesus said unto him, Thou shalt love the Lord thy God with all thy heart, and with all thy soul, and with all thy mind. This is the first and great commandment. And the second is like unto it, Thou shalt love thy neighbor as thyself. On these two commandments hang all the law and the prophets. (Matthew 22:37–40)

And every one that heareth these sayings of mine, and doeth them not, shall be likened unto a foolish man, which built his house upon the sand: And the rain descended, and the floods came, and the winds blew, and beat upon that house; and it fell: and great was the fall of it. (Matthew 7:26–27)

I pray that you will recognize that your strength comes from the Lord (Isaiah 40:29; Philippians 4:13). May God give us the power to fight the evil of our day, even if this results in death.

STUMBLING

Here in Canada, we are reverting to a modified Stage 2 in the COVID-19 fight. Many people have experienced ups and downs in life. Sometimes taking a step backward is necessary, to regain our footing so we can move forward stronger.

Jesus took a step backward. He went from being filled with the glory of God and dwelling daily in God's presence to suffering on Earth. He willingly gave that all up in order to gain with his own blood a secure footing for mankind. Consider His prayer:

> Father, the hour has come. Glorify your Son, that your Son may glorify you. For you granted him authority over all people that he might give eternal life to all those you have given him. Now this is eternal life: that they know you, the only true God, and Jesus Christ, whom you have sent. I have brought you glory on earth by finishing the work you gave me to do. And now, Father, glorify me in your presence with the glory I had with you before the world began. (Matthew 17:2–5)

In your relationships with one another, have the same mindset as Christ Jesus: Who, being in very nature God, did not consider equality with God something to be used to his own advantage; rather, he made himself nothing by taking the very nature of a servant, being made in human likeness. And being found in appearance as a man, he humbled himself by becoming obedient to death – even death on a cross! (Philippians 2:5–8 NIV)

If Jesus took a step back, certainly we can too. Are you willing to take a step back in order to grow spiritually? Are you willing to humble yourself? "Humble yourselves, therefore, under God's mighty hand, that he may lift you up in due time" (1 Peter 5:6 NIV).

There is nothing more humbling than repenting. Accepting that you have done wrong, feeling sorry for the wrong done and acquiring a true desire to change. This will require stopping certain activities and starting new ones. Do this and God's promise is He will lift you up in due time.

There is no telling the highs you can gain when your paths are ordered by God. There are several promises regarding this in the Bible and they are wonderful. Here is one: "In their hearts humans plan their course, but the LORD establishes their steps" (Proverbs 16:9 NIV).

Let the Lord establish your steps. Take a step back, look at your life, and determine how you will move forward. I pray it is in humility, following the example of Christ – denying Himself, so others might be the beneficiaries.

In the end, you will benefit in same way as Jesus will. He will be crowned King of Kings and Lord of Lords. And if you overcome, you will reign with him, sit on his throne, and eat at his table:

> To the one who is victorious, I will give the right to sit with me on my throne, just as I was victorious and sat down with my Father on his throne. (Revelation 3:21 NIV)

Faith – in His Promises

Blessed are the poor in spirit, for theirs is the kingdom of heaven. (Matthew 5:3)

God has made many promises to the poor. Remember, God is not slack concerning his promises, and neither can he lie (Titus 1:2). His words can be taken to the bank of our minds and be deposited. When King David said, "I have never seen the righteous forsaken or their children begging bread" (Psalm 37:25 NIV), we need to understand what he meant. The answer is found in the great sermon Jesus preached on the mount:

> Therefore, take no thought, saying, what shall we eat? Or what shall we drink? Or Wherewithal shall we be clothed? For your heavenly Father knows that ye have need of all these things. But seek ye first the kingdom of God, and his righteousness; and all these things shall be added unto you. (Matthew 6:31–32)

God regards you as his responsibility. That is why he says, "Whoever is kind to the poor lends to God" (Proverbs 19:4).

Other promises of His say the following:

> When the poor and needy seek water, and there is none, and their tongue faileth for thirst, I the LORD will hear them, I the God of Israel will not forsake them. I will open rivers in high places, and fountains in the midst of the valleys: I will make the wilderness a pool of water, and the dry land springs of water. (Isaiah 41:17–18)

> I know that the LORD will maintain the cause of the afflicted, and the right of the poor. (Psalm 140:12)

Do not think for a minute that you have been forsaken by God. You may not have many earthly possessions, but there is one possession that remains: your life. To the rich, God commands the following: "Give all you have to the poor and come and follow me." Many possessions hold back the rich from following God, but there is nothing holding the poor back. All of us, rich and poor, come into the world naked and we all leave with nothing.

When we came into the world, we came with life. This is ours to keep if we will. It is this life that Jesus refers to in the parable of the talents as the thing that will be taken away from the wicked and lazy servant:

> For unto every one that hath shall be given, and he

shall have abundance: but from him that hath not shall be taken away even that which he hath. And cast ye the unprofitable servant into outer darkness: there shall be weeping and gnashing of teeth. (Matthew 25:29–30)

The great patriarch Abraham was willing to give up his prized possession, his son, to follow God. God was willing to give up his prized possession, Jesus his son, to save us from sin and death.

Will you give up your own life to follow God? Is not that all which remains? What do you have to lose? Earthly possessions, family, friends?

Seek God first, and everything else will be added unto you. His Word, his character, and reputation are at stake. Try him and see the results. Humble yourself before God, and inherit the kingdom of heaven.

Will you follow him today?

CREATION

SCIENCE AND EVOLUTION IN CRISIS

Our situation with COVID-19 has created a divide on several issues. There is a divide of opinions concerning the legality of lockdowns, the economy, mandatory vaccines, individual rights versus the public good. These are difficult issues. An undertone among them all is the spiritual implications - our God-given rights or lack thereof.

There has long been a debate between creation and evolution, but now we are pressed to obey the experts – *the scientists* – on issues that will have a far-reaching impact on us, our families, and the world. These experts teach that human beings are a random product of time plus matter plus chance. If we are held in such low esteem, can we trust scientists as our decision-makers?

The spiritual issue that underscores everything occurring in the world is the question "Is God the Creator?" This is a moral question. It is important because God holds human beings in high esteem. The Bible states the following about human beings:

- Man was made in the image of God (Genesis 1:27)

- Man has the ability to have the fullness of God dwell within (Ephesians 3:19)

- Man, made temporarily a little lower than angels, is crowned with glory and honor. (Psalm 8:4–5)

The creation week in Genesis consist of six creation days, and one rest day. The Bible states that "one day is with the Lord as a thousand years, and a thousand years as one day." (Psalm 90:4; 2 Peter 3:8). The Bible teaches that human history is unfolding along a timeline of only 7,000 years, the final 1,000 years consisting of a reign with God and Christ. (Revelation 20:6).

Day	What Was Created	Results	Timeline
1	Light and Darkness	Adam and Even covered with the light of God, but then they sinned. Adam died at the age of 930.	~ 4000 BC
2	Firmament	Noah and warning of the flood. Noah lived for 950 years.	~ 3000 BC
3	Dry Land, Seeds, and Plants	Abrahamic covenant fulfilled, with Moses and the exodus.	~ 2000 BC
4	Sun, Moon, and Stars	Promise of Christ, birth, and death of Christ.	~ 1000 BC
5	Life: Birds, Sea Animals	The message of Christ is preached for eternal life. Beast of the sea.	~ 1000 A.D.
6	Life: Land Animals and Humans	The destruction of the image of God in man. The beast of the earth. The mark of the beast / Antichrist / man of sin	~ 2000 AD
7	Sabbath Rest	Millennium of rest	~ 3000 AD

The above chart shows a highlight of the events of human history to our current time.

We cannot waver between two opinions indefinitely. Either God is the Creator and we ought to follow him, or we are a product of random chance, and our choices are inconsequential. What choice will you make? Is God the Creator? If yes, will you follow him and trust his word, as revealed in the Bible?

I hope you choose to obey God and Christ, so you will reign with him in his throne for 1,000 years.

LAWS OF HEALTH

"In the beginning God created the heavens and the earth" (Genesis 1:1). For this reason, God is referred to as the Creator:

> Do you not know? Have you not heard?
> The LORD is the everlasting God,
> the Creator of the ends of the earth.
> He will not grow tired or weary,
> and his understanding no one can fathom.
> He gives strength to the weary and increases
> the power of the weak. (Isaiah 40:40–29 NIV)

The building blocks of life (proteins, ribosomes, enzymes, etc.) are formed at the direction of specific nucleotide sequencing in DNA. DNA sequencing contains information for the creation of proteins required by every organ in the body. The information required for life precedes life itself. This is a challenge for atheists or others who believe in a random, chance event that brought life into existence. Compounding this problem are the two concepts Mitochondrial Eve and Y-chromosomal Adam. These, based on certain assumptions, point to a single original man and woman who lived approximately 6,000 years ago.

With the advances in modern technology, we can analyze DNA and RNA to understand how they work. These advances have led scientists to create experimental instructions (mRNA) to direct cells to make specific spike proteins. This is an amazing accomplishment of modern medicine. However, it assumes that our everlasting, all-knowing Creator requires the help of humans or that humans can do a better job.

Sickness according to the Bible has three primary causes. The first is sin (Psalm 38:3; Micah 6:13; 1 Corinthians 11:30). The second is that the works of God may be displayed (John 9:3). The third is due to being a horrible steward to our body. All causes apply to us today, however our present situation is most likely here that the works of God may be displayed.

Why? Because those who trust either in men's creations or those who trust in God's processes (Genesis 1:29) will have to deal with the outcome of their decisions. This warning was given long ago:

> Fear God and give him glory, because the hour of his judgment has come. Worship him who made the heavens, the earth, the sea and the springs of water. (Revelation 14:7)

The glory of God is man (1 Corinthians 11:7). To give him glory is to reserve our bodies for him by obeying his commands. Then God will use our bodies for his glorious works.

Job is an example of a sick person in the Bible, in whom the works of God were displayed. He lost his health, wife, children, and all his possessions after the devil caused him to suffer. However, Job trusted in his Creator and never waivered in his stand for God, uttering the words "Though he slay me, yet will I trust him."

His faith in his Creator was rewarded. Everything he lost was doubly restored. Whom will you trust? Will you trust in men and the new experimental mRNA or will you trust in God?

I pray you will, before making a life-altering decision, consider whom to trust. As for me, I know my that "my redeemer lives, and that in the end he will stand on the earth" (Job 19:25).

SELF-CONTROL

POWER OF WORDS

The summer has gone and so has time, it seems. Every day seems more squeezed, perhaps it's the early retirement of the sun. The line up to exit my street has grown, delaying arrival at my destination. Now it's all about the busy schedule, with back to work and back to school; it's now about the huge balancing act. We all need to continually learn, so when we see students heading back to school we wonder how much wiser they will become next summer. One of the most important lessons I have learned is the power in spoken words.

This past weekend I was reminded of that fact. Many of us from very early in our lives placed labels on ourselves, some more sinister than others. We may even do it unwittingly as if we did not have a choice in the matter. I am a smoker, I am stupid, I am . . . etc. These labels limit us, and now we see our life from the lenses of a smoker, or a stupid person, and we may even compound it by our actions. For example, I can't stay in this hotel as there are no rooms for smokers, I am too stupid to ever get that job or start my own business. Imagine for a minute that if every person heading back to school this fall said I am a failure, all who proclaimed such words would either fail or drop out before completing.

I encourage you to read James 3:1–6:

> Not many of you should become teachers, my fellow believers, because you know that we who teach will be judged more strictly. We all stumble in many ways. Anyone who is never at fault in what they say is perfect, able to keep their whole body in check.
>
> When we put bits into the mouths of horses to make them obey us, we can turn the whole animal. Or take ships as an example. Although they are so large and are driven by strong winds, they are steered by a very small rudder wherever the pilot wants to go. Likewise, the tongue is a small part of the body, but it makes great boasts. Consider what a great forest is set on fire by a small spark. The tongue also is a fire, a world of evil among the parts of the body. It corrupts the whole body, sets the whole course of one's life on fire, and is itself set on fire by hell. (James 3:1–6 NIV)

Understand the power of spoken words, as they set our whole life course. If that be the case, then we need to change our conversation with our loved ones, our children, our families and friends. We need to be cognizant of the words we speak and display a new level of self-control. Why is this important?

> Where no wood is, there the fire goeth out: so where there is no talebearer, the strife ceaseth. (Proverbs 26:20)

Let's say only good things about our neighbors, coworkers, family, friends, and acquaintances. Let's make our community the most loving, and we can do that by adjusting our words. By changing the words we speak, all strife will cease in our homes and community, and endless possibilities for a bright future will emerge.

Today, to everyone reading this letter the call is – let's declare that there be Love, Joy, and Peace.

I hope you found value in the sharing of an important lesson I have learned: our words have the power to create:

> Death and life are in the power of the tongue, and those who love it will eat its fruits. (Proverbs 18:21)

Choose life!

PROPHECY

New World Order and Sin

Are you concerned about the rapid changes occurring in society? It seems like every day there is a new headline in the news about a terrorist attack, a public shooting, riots, or violence. The changes occurring in our society today are unlike anything we have ever seen. Every branch of government is pressing to remain relevant, politically correct, and able to respond to the latest trend in the news – whether it be LGBTQ issues, race relations, immigrants, gun control, education, fiscal responsibility, or our current freedoms.

These issues and tensions will become magnified as each citizen chooses a stand on the various issues facing society. Such a choice will further escalate tensions, making them unbearable and requiring outside help to resolve. People are becoming depressed at a higher rate: 10% of Canadians 15 years and older will have symptoms of mental or substance abuse disorders in the next 12 months.

Society will make you believe that we are progressing, becoming better than our previous selves, attaining to the next step in the evolutionary understanding of the world, as we enter Earth's next phase, or "new world order." In the new order there is no place for God, rule of law, or public expression of our views, especially the unpopular ones.

There is an answer to these questions, an answer to the situations the world is entangled with and an answer to future crises on the horizon. Whether they be from the Zika virus or financial uncertainty, we know another crisis is not far away. Many times we feel we have to look south of the border, but there is enough drama locally. Just look at the condition of our family relationships between brother and sister, husband and wife, stepfather and stepmother – there is more than enough happening here to make us realize we need help.

However unpopular it may be, the Bible holds the answer: James 4:1–4 says:

> From whence *come* wars and fightings among you? *come they* not hence, *even* of your lusts that war in your members? Ye lust, and have not: ye kill, and desire to have, and cannot obtain: ye fight and war, yet ye have not, because ye ask not. Ye ask, and receive not, because ye ask amiss, that ye may consume *it* upon your lusts. Ye adulterers and adulteresses, know ye not that the friendship of the world is enmity with God? whosoever therefore will be a friend of the world is the enemy of God.

In current times many of our problems come from lust. We lust for more of everything: money, real estate, sexual pleasure, drugs, or alcohol, but they do not fulfill our needs. We only seem to want more, in a vicious cycle that usually leads to abuse, drug abuse, alcohol abuse, sexual abuse, financial ruin, etc.

The Bible says we ask and receive not because we only ask to consume, and to consume upon our lusts. This is absolutely true in our present day, when ideas of delayed gratification are non-existent. Going even further, the Bible says sins starts with lust:

James 1:13–15 says:

> Let no man say when he is tempted, I am tempted of God: for God cannot be tempted with evil, neither tempteth he any man: But every man is tempted, when he is drawn away of his own lust, and enticed. Then when lust hath conceived, it bringeth forth sin: and sin, when it is finished, bringeth forth death.

The devil is out to seek and destroy and is the main culprit behind all our problems today. However, the devil does not have any power to force any of our actions: we are responsible for our own actions.

As a neighbor, I encourage you to flee from his presence, temptations, and nongodly, evil desires. Resist the devil and he will flee from you. Finally, James 4:7–10 says:

Submit yourselves therefore to God. Resist the devil, and he will flee from you. Draw nigh to God, and he will draw nigh to you. Cleanse *your* hands, *ye* sinners; and purify *your* hearts, *ye* double minded. Be afflicted, and mourn, and weep: let your laughter be turned to mourning, and *your* joy to heaviness. Humble yourselves in the sight of the Lord, and he shall lift you up.

The solution to every problem is simple: submit to God and resist the devil. If you have neglected to do this in the past, I encourage you to hold your family members' hands tonight, pray, confess your sins to God, and seek his will.

John 6:37 says, whoever turns to God he will not turn away.

Have a wonderful evening and may you see bright mornings, with a renewed joy for life.

ABOMINATION OF DESOLATION

Referring to a future time, Jesus warns about the "abomination of desolation": "When ye therefore shall see the abomination of desolation, spoken of by Daniel the prophet, stand in the holy place, then let them which be in Judaea flee into the mountains" (Matthew 24:15).

In Luke's Gospel, more color is provided: the sign is listed as Jerusalem being surrounded by armies (Luke 21:20–24). What is the abomination of desolation? What happened historically in Jerusalem? Why is this important for believers in Jesus Christ?

An abomination is a gross sin, punishable by death (Deuteronomy 18:12; Proverbs 6:16–19; Ezekiel 16:22). Chiefly among these sins are idolatry, sexual sins, and shedding innocent blood. The desolation or death of the guilty is the result of these sins (Leviticus 18:24). The gross sin the Jewish nation committed was the killing of Jesus the Christ (Matthew 23:37–38). Here we have an abomination – shedding of innocent blood – which resulted in death and the desolation of

Jerusalem in AD 70. Daniel the prophet prophesied this event in amazing detail:

> And after threescore and two weeks shall Messiah be cut off, but not for himself: and the people of the prince that shall come shall destroy the city and the sanctuary; and the end thereof shall be with a flood, and unto the end of the war desolations are determined. (Daniel 9:26)

Daniel explained that Titus – without calling him by name – would destroy Jerusalem. Today, there is no physical temple as the last temple was destroyed in AD 70. Christian bodies are now the temple where Jesus resides (Acts 7:48; 1 Corinthians 16:9). Jesus promised to dwell in every believer's heart by his Holy Spirit, as shown in 2 Corinthians 13:5, Romans 8:10, Galatians 2:20, and many more verses in the Bible.

We commit the same sin as the Jews by rejecting Jesus Christ, replacing him with idols and engaging in abominable practices. Our society commits these abominable sins by shedding innocent blood, indulging in various kinds of deviant sexual behavior, and rejecting the liberating role Christ has in the proper functioning of society.

Without accepting Jesus and his shed blood, which clears the guilty (1 John 1:7–9), we have our own lives to pay for the consequence of sin: "For the wages of sin is death; but the gift of God is eternal life through Jesus Christ our Lord" (Romans 6:23).

In AD 70 many Christians, seeing the promised warning signs, escaped from Jerusalem to Pella and saved their lives and those of their families. Today if we heed the same warning, we can save our lives too. The temple – our bodies – will become "desolate," just like the temple in Jerusalem became desolate during the AD 70 invasion of Titus if we fail to listen.

This was final warning for the people of God in Jerusalem and will be the final warning for us.

Book of Revelation

Have you tried reading the book of Revelation? If you read it, you may have found it difficult to understand. The book of Revelation offers a blessing for those who read it aloud. For this reason alone, it is worth reading. The first thing to understand when reading any book of the Bible is to realize the subject is Jesus. This is consistent in Revelation and is a key to understanding the book:

> Search the scriptures; for in them ye think ye have eternal life: and they are they which testify of me [Jesus]. (John 5:39)

> In the past God spoke to our ancestors through the prophets at many times and in various ways, but in these last days he has spoken to us by his Son, whom he appointed heir of all things, and through whom also he made the universe. (Hebrews 1:2)

> The Revelation from Jesus Christ, which God gave

unto him, to shew unto his servants things which must shortly come to pass; and he sent and signified it by his angel unto his servant John. (Revelation 1:1)

The book of Revelation is Jesus speaking directly to us, telling us the things that should come to pass, revealing his work. Prior to Jesus first coming, it was prophesied that when he comes, he will speak in parables:

I will open my mouth in a parable: I will utter dark sayings of old. (Psalm 78:2)

Jesus spoke all these things to the crowd in parables; he did not say anything to them without using a parable. So was fulfilled what was spoken through the prophet: "I will open my mouth in parables, I will utter things hidden since the creation of the world." (Matthew 13:34–35 NIV)

John wrote the book of Revelation, recording what he was told and what he saw in visions from Jesus (Revelation 1:11). The parable language Jesus used in the past continues in the book of Revelation. The second key to understanding Revelation is to understand what these symbols mean. The Bible is consistent: symbols mean the same thing throughout. For example, a woman, used throughout the book of Revelation, represents the church, either the pure church of God or, in contrast, the corrupt church.

The purpose of Revelation is to echo the last message of warning, "for the time is at hand," and point us to Jesus' soon return" "I am coming soon! My reward is with me, and I will give to each person according to what they have done" (Revelation 22:12 NIV).

Next time you read Revelation, keep in mind there is a blessing for reading aloud, it is all about Jesus and the work he is doing, it uses symbolic, not literal, language, it is written for our present-day, and it delivers the last message of warning: "Blessed is the one who reads aloud the words of this prophecy and blessed are those who hear it and take to heart what is written in it, because the time is near" (Revelation 1:3 NIV).

The Mark of the Beast

The crisis deepens and many are now questioning if this is the *mark of the beast* the Bible talks about. To understand the mark of the beast we must understand the creation story. On the sixth day of creation, God created man and the beasts of the fields. This is where six as the number of a man, finds its origin (Revelation 13:18).

The importance of creation is twofold. First, it identifies God as creator, and second it identifies us as being made in his image (Genesis 1:27). This is the truth about God that many have exchange for a lie and, instead of worshiping God as Creator, many have chosen to worship man and created things (Romans 1:25). In doing so, they have made void the law of God.

Worship is the key to understanding the mark of the beast. Worship means allegiance:

> And the third angel followed them, saying with a loud voice, If any man worship the beast and his image, and receive his mark in his forehead, or in his hand, The same shall drink of the wine of the wrath of God,

which is poured out without mixture into the cup of his indignation; and he shall be tormented with fire and brimstone in the presence of the holy angels, and in the presence of the Lamb. Revelation 14:9–10

A clear passage to understand this is found in Mark, where Jesus says to them, "Give back to Caesar what is Caesar's and to God what is God's" (Mark 12:17). What is due to God is our worship of him as the Creator because his image is on all of us. Worship is the keeping of God's commandments (Mark 7:13), and the first four – one God, no graven images, reverence of his Name, reverence of his seventh day – will be counterfeited by the beast of Revelation.

Worship is more than attendance at and participation in church services. It is giving our all to God without limits. Our all means our bodies, and our spirit. The Bible says those who worship God must worship him in spirit and in truth. During creation God first formed the body and then added the spirit by blowing into the nostrils of Adam, the first man. The Bible says the Christian's body is the temple of God (1 Corinthians 16:9) in which his Spirit dwells. Truth is found in Jesus, the Word of God (John 14:6).

Daniel, a prominent Bible character, while in captivity refused to defile his body with the king's food, and his spirit with the king's laws (Daniel 1:8; 6). This he did as an act of worship, believing that obedience to God was better than eating the delicacies of the king. We today have the same option before us: Will we be obedient and faithful to God or will we worship the beast and its image? This requires diligence, as many will be deceived into receiving the mark of the beast (Revelation 19:20).

The choice to worship God as creator will become increasingly difficult, as refusal to worship the beast will result in exclusion from the economy – buying and selling – and death (Revelation 13:15, 17). The time ahead of us will be trying for Bible-believing Christians. So difficult in fact that it is questioned whether Jesus will find anyone faithful living on Earth when he returns (Luke 18:8)?

Take courage, for we have many precious promises to hold on to. We do not need to be afraid of those who kill the body, because as God raised Jesus from the dead so he promises to raise his followers from the dead. When we can no longer buy or sell, we can be certain God will provide for our needs as he does for the birds, and as he did for Israel as they traveled to the Promised Land.

CHURCH AND STATE

Do you remember what happened during the Dark Ages? The unity of church and state led to the persecution of Bible-believing Christians. Today such Christians are nominally called fundamentalists. In the Dark Ages the light of the Bible slowly extinguished in society due to the suppression of the truth. As prophesied in the book of Daniel, chapter 7, the little horn did speak pompous words against the Most High and the holy people were delivered into this hands for the allotted period of time (1,260 years). During this period millions of God's true commandment-keeping people were martyred for refusing to follow the dictates of the Roman Church.

Christians were forced to yield their integrity and accept the papal ceremonies and worship, or wear away their lives in dungeons or suffer death. Now were fulfilled the words of Jesus "Ye shall be betrayed both by parents, and brethren, and kinsfolks, and friends; and some of you shall they cause to be put to death. And ye shall be hated of all men for My name's sake"

(Luke 21:16–17).

Fortunately, this time period of history ended.

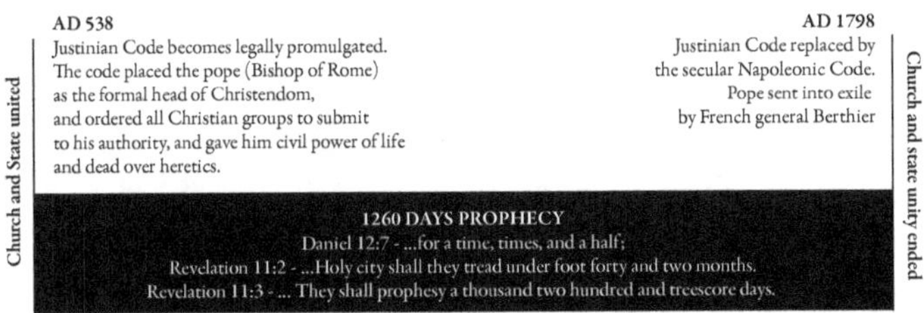

Napoleon's general Berthier captured the pope. France's intention was another pope would never be crowned. Berthier was the hand that delivered the deadly wound to fulfill the word of God. It is important to note that the wound would not kill but, as foretold, the wound would heal. This healing occurred gradually. Several events that occurred recently point to the healing of the wound:

- The celebrated end of the Protestant Reformation in 2019
- The pope's address to the US Congress in 2015

Today the papacy has taken a leading role in climate change. The Bible predicts a revival of the papacy will occur in the last days, which will lead the world to unfollow biblical teachings. The Bible says the whole world will marvel and follow after the beast, and encourages us to come out of her *my people.*

Will you follow the beast and false prophet, or will you follow the Light of the world, the true and living God?

PROPHECY – ANARCHY

Anarchy is among us. ANTIFA, Anti-Fascism, which sounds good in principle, is blamed for wreaking havoc in the US and Canada. Hitler's government is an example of a fascist government. In Montreal a legitimate protest was hijacked, and businesses destroyed. While it may sound good, this AN-TIFA movement is powered by lawlessness and is deceiving many. Jesus asked a potent question: "Can Satan drive out Satan?" (Mark 3:23).

Lucifer attempted to usurp the government of God when he started a rebellion in heaven. He was kicked out, but found a place on Earth:

> And there was war in heaven: Michael and his angels fought against the dragon; and the dragon fought and his angels, And prevailed not; neither was their place found any more in heaven. And the great dragon was cast out, that old serpent, called the Devil, and Satan, which deceiveth the whole world: he was cast out into the earth, and his angels were cast out with him. (Rev-

elation 12:7–9)

The devil then craftily tempted Eve by saying, "Did God really say?"

This same spirit of the devil remains at work in the world. Not only are God's laws being violated, but human laws are now being cast aside. The spirit of the Satan is at work: the spirit of anarchy, strife, hatred, and division. This is in stark contrast to the fruits of the Holy Spirit: love, joy, peace, patience, kindness, goodness, faithfulness, gentleness, and self-control, against which there are no laws (Galatians 5:22).

A war between good and evil is raging widely in our world. We can be either victors or causalities. If we fight on the side of Satan using his weapons of lawlessness, division, and hatred to one another, we and Satan will lose. If we fight on God's side using his weapons, we will win:

> For though we walk in the flesh, we do not war after the flesh: (For the weapons of our warfare are not carnal, but mighty through God to the pulling down of strong holds; Casting down imaginations, and every high thing that exalteth itself against the knowledge of God, and bringing into captivity every thought to the obedience of Christ; (Corinthians 10:4–5)

> Put on the full armor of God, so that you can take

your stand against the devil's schemes. For our struggle is not against flesh and blood, but against the rulers, against the authorities, against the powers of this dark world and against the spiritual forces of evil in the heavenly realms. Therefore, put on the full armor of God, so that when the day of evil comes, you may be able to stand your ground, and after you have done everything, to stand. (Ephesians 11–13)

Which side will you fight on? Matthew 21:44 shares two options: "And whoever shall fall on this stone shall be broken: but on whomsoever it shall fall, it will grind him to powder." Christ is the stone, the chief cornerstone upon whom we ought to build our hopes and lives. Doing so requires us to be broken from earthly hopes and dreams. Like Abraham, we are to look forward to the heavenly city, with heavenly goals and dreams. Alternatively, we can prioritize earthly passions, and lose out on God's kingdom and be destroyed.

INFLATION AND MONEY

The price of gas has reached a record high and is expected to increase more. Likewise, food prices have increased in line with the message of Revelation: "Two pounds of wheat for a day's wages, and six pounds of barley for a day's wages, and do not damage the oil and the wine!" (Revelation 6:6 NIV).

The children of Israel became salves in Egypt for want of food. They used their money first to buy food, then their animals, followed by their land. With nothing remaining, they became slaves:

> Surely we will die while you are watching. But if you give us food, we will give Pharaoh our land, and we will be his slaves. Give us seed so that we can plant. Then we will live and not die, and the land will grow food for us again. (Genesis 47:19 NLT)

These events are repeating, for there is nothing new under the sun (Ecclesiastes 1:9). We are warned that a time of trouble is coming upon us, prior to the coming of Jesus Christ. Jesus says, "Come unto me, all who labor and are heaven laden, and I will give you rest" (Matthew 11:28). Jesus found food by doing the will of his father (John 4:34). Jesus also promises we will never thirst by drinking the water he provides (John 4:14). "He shall dwell on high: his place of defence shall be the munitions of rocks: bread shall be given him; his waters shall be sure" (Isaiah 33:16).

These things will happen – the Bible is God's Word, and God cannot lie (Hebrews 6:18)! Our duty is to prepare for these events. We do not need to work, as Jesus has already completed the work on our behalf, we only need to trust in his completed work, and allow him in to work within us.

In Exodus 20, Moses is given the Ten Commandments. God reminds us in the fourth commandment that he is the creator of heaven and Earth. In Deuteronomy 5, after the children of Israel have exited Egypt, they are reminded again of the Ten Commandments. In the fourth commandment, they are reminded that God is their Redeemer. He is the Redeemer because he has taken the people out of slavery from Egypt. For these two reasons, God as Creator and God as Redeemer, we ought to rest from our own work and observe the Sabbath – the seventh day of the week or Saturday. The seventh day points to God's completed work as Creator and Redeemer.

Jesus says come unto to me all who are labouring and are tired. As Creator, God owns all the resources of this Earth. As redeemer, he owns you and me:

> I know every bird in the mountains, and the creatures of the field are mine.
> If I were hungry I would not tell you,
> for the world is mine, and all that is in it. (Psalm 50:12, 13 NIV)

> It is for freedom that Christ has set us free. Stand firm, then, and do not let yourselves be burdened again by a yoke of slavery. (Galatians 5:1 NIV)

> Do not fear, I have told you now before it happens, so that when it does happen you will believe. (John 14:29)

> When you see these things happen look up because your redemption is drawing near. (Luke 21:28)

For six thousand years (Act 17:26), the great controversy between good and evil has unfolded. Now it is wrapping up and we ought to do the work Christ commands and trust in his completed work and all his promises.

Acknowledge him by resting in his completed work as he commands. "It is God who works in you to will and to act in order to fulfill his good purpose" (Philippians 2:13 NIV).

"If anyone hears my voice and opens the door, I will come in and eat with that person, and they with me" (Revelation 3:20 NIV).

INFLATION AND WORLD EVENTS

As each day passes, our world becomes more unstable. The policies implemented in response to the coronavirus has caused many to lose their jobs from lockdowns. The job losses in turn caused an increased dependency on the government for financial support. A new measure – vaccine mandates – is adding to the supply crisis as many essential workers are placed on leave and may ultimately lose their jobs if they do not comply. Inflation is increasing at a rate unseen in Western societies. Our government is indebted to a degree that was previously unimaginable. As our debt increases our independence decreases.

Speaking of inflation, "Two pounds of wheat for a day's wages, and six pounds of barley for a day's wages, and do not damage the oil and the wine!" (Revelation 6:6 NIV). Imagine a bag of flour for a day's wages! Are you ready for the financial crisis?

Proverbs says, "The rich ruleth over the poor, and the borrower is servant to the lender" (Proverbs 22:7 NIV). Who is the lender to our government? The Bible gives an answer:

> For all nations have drunk of the wine of the wrath of her fornication, and the kings of the earth have committed fornication with her, and the merchants of the earth are waxed rich through the abundance of her delicacies. And I heard another voice from heaven, saying, Come out of her, my people, that ye be not partakers of her sins, and that ye receive not of her plagues. (Revelation 18:3–5)

These events are accumulating and will result in a historic financial and political event, sooner than we can imagine. We are called to come out of Babylon and not partake of her sins. Esau for a single meal sold his inheritance rights as the oldest son (Hebrews 12:16); likewise, many will forfeit heaven for food or a job and accept the mark of the beast.

The Bible warns of these things that are occurring today, in the last days of earth history: "Go to now, ye rich men, weep and howl for your miseries that shall come upon you. Your riches are corrupted, and your garments are motheaten" (James 1:1–2).

The governments of this world will wail, and lament. God's words and judgment are sure. We are called to put our reliance on God, and not man (Psalm 146:3–4). We are called to obey the Word of God, and are promised that he will provide us food and shelter:

> Therefore take no thought, saying, What shall we eat? or, What shall we drink? or, Wherewithal shall we be clothed? (For after all these things do the Gentiles seek:) for your heavenly Father knoweth that ye have need of all these things. But seek ye first the kingdom of God, and his righteousness; and all these things shall be added unto you. (Matthew 6:32–33)

"Come out of her my people" is the call. Come out of her, and run to the one true God – Jesus, Christ our Righteousness. Only in him can you be safe from the things coming upon this world. Come out, before it is too late.

Who/What Is Babylon?

Revelation 17 describes Babylon in detail. Babylon is used symbolically. It parallels the city of Babylon in the Old Testament. The same city where Daniel and the Israelites were held as captives. Ancient Babylon erected a golden image of a man and forced the people to worship the image or face death. Babylon represents the cities of the world today who force their populace to violate their conscience. It represents the great city, which is also the harlot, the false mother of churches (*a woman represents a church; i.e. the bride of Christ*).

In Revelation Babylon represents all who do not worship the true and living God. It represents all who persecute believers who *do* worship the God who in seven literal days created the heaven and earth, the sea, and the fountains of water. Babylon means confusion. It represents all religions that claim to worship God, but do not in fact obey him. It represents the Roman Church, and its persecution of those who obey God according to dictates of their conscience. Babylon's daughters are Protestant churches that reject Bible truth and assault those who accept it.

THE SANCTUARY

THE SANCTUARY – WHERE IS JESUS?

Have you ever wondered where Jesus is? His return has now been promised for over 2000 years. How can Christians still hold hope that he will come? "The Lord is not slack concerning His promise, as some count slackness, but is longsuffering toward us, not willing that any should perish but that all should come to repentance" (2 Peter 3:9).

To understand where Jesus is, and what he is doing, a sound understanding of historical events is required. These historical events foreshadow the future events of Jesus.

Prior to his first coming to earth, Jesus was in heaven with God the Father (John 1:1): "I have brought you glory on earth by finishing the work you gave me to do. And now, Father, glorify me in your presence with the glory I had with you before the world began" (John 17:4 NIV).

Before creation, Jesus was with the Father. During creation, he was present (1 Colossians 1:16), during the time of Abraham he was present (John 8:56–58), and during the time of Moses and the exodus he was present (1 Corinthians 10:1–4).

When the priesthood was established, the sanctuary was erected to point to a future work Jesus had to complete:

> Thy way, O God, is in the sanctuary:
>
> who is so great a God as our God? (Psalm 77:13).

The sanctuary on earth, famously represented first in Solomon's and then in Herod's temple, was made according to the pattern of a preexisting sanctuary in heaven (Exodus 25:9; Joshua 22:28). The sanctuary was divided into three areas: the courtyard, the holy place and the most holy place. The tribes of Israel camped around the sanctuary, with Judah to the east, at the entrance of the sanctuary. It is out of this tribe that Jesus was born – the Lion of the tribe of Judah.

Jesus made his way, doing according to all the Scriptures said, into the sanctuary and was crucified as the Lamb of God for the sins of the world. Historically the sacrificing of animals occurred in the courtyard. The holy place and the most holy place are where the high priest did his work. In terms of Jesus' life, the courtyard is on Earth, where he died, and the holy place and most holy place are in heaven.

Jesus explained his purpose many times to his listeners:

> For I have come down from heaven not to do my will but to do *the will of him who sent me.* (John 6:38 NIV)

He said to them, "Why did you seek Me? Did you

not know that *I must be about My Father's business?*"
(Luke 2:49 NASB 1977)

Father, if thou be willing, remove this cup from me:
nevertheless *not my will, but thine, be done.* (Luke
22:42)

The purpose of Jesus' life on earth was to do the Father's
will – to be the sacrifice for sin. To understand what Jesus is doing now, we need to know what the high priest did historically
in the temple.

After his death, Jesus explained to his disciples, beginning
with Moses and all the prophets, what was said in the Scriptures about himself (Luke 24:27).

This was the start of Jesus' work as our High Priest. In due
time, as he continued his work, he moved from the holy place
to the most holy place to begin the judgment: "Therefore, since
we have a great high priest who has ascended into heaven, Jesus
the Son of God, let us hold firmly to the faith we profess" (Hebrews 4:14 NIV).

Today, Jesus is ministering in the heavenly sanctuary as our
high priest. While he is ministering in the sanctuary, we have
an opportunity to have our sins forgiven by his shed blood.

By the which will we are sanctified through the offering of the body of Jesus Christ once for all. And every

priest standeth daily ministering and offering often-times the same sacrifices, which can never take away sins: But this man, after he had offered one sacrifice for sins for ever, sat down on the right hand of God; From henceforth expecting till his enemies be made his footstool. (Hebrews 10:10–13)

Are you still wondering, where Jesus is? He is in heaven, doing his Father's will. His next move is to leave the most holy place in the heavenly sanctuary and return to earth: "'Men of Galilee,' they said, 'why do you stand here looking into the sky? This same Jesus, who has been taken from you into heaven, will come back in the same way you have seen him go into heaven'" (Acts 1:11).

"Therefore, as we have opportunity, let us do good to all people, especially to those who belong to the family of believers" (Galatians 6:10). Let us do the Father's will.

God is not slack concerning his promises: Jesus *will* return.

The State
of the Dead

UFOs and UAP

Recently, there has been an increased interest in aliens, unidentified flying objects (UFOs), and unidentified aerial phenomena (UAP). The Pentagon released a report on UAPs. The pope commented he would baptize Martians or any aliens that showed up at the Vatican and asked for it. The Mutual UFO Network (MUFON), founded in 1969, has thousands of UFO sightings and alien abduction stories in their database. What are we to make of these events and what does the Bible say about them?

Many would be overwhelmed with fear if they were to see an alien, or if they were abducted. Second Timothy 1:7 says, "For God hath not given us a spirit of fear; but of power, and of love, and of a sound mind." The Bible also comforts us by letting us know that at the name of Jesus every knee will bow, in heaven and on earth and under the earth (Philippians 2:10). The MUFON database confirms that those being abducted who call on the name of Jesus for help cause the abductions promptly to end.

Aliens are demons. Demons are evil spirits, fallen angels, and those who have seen them are witnesses to the evil influences that surround us. Many are unwittingly inviting these spirits into their homes. Those who are involved with the occult are more likely to be abducted by aliens and witness the manifestation of these evil beings. Ephesians 5:11 warns us to have nothing to do with the fruitless deeds of darkness, but rather to expose them.

Aliens are subjected to God's will. "And, behold, they [*evil spirits*] cried out, saying, What have we to do with thee, Jesus, thou Son of God? art thou come hither to torment us before the time?" (Matthew 8:29). There is a time established for the destruction of all evil. All evildoers will be cast into everlasting fire prepared for the devil and his angels (Matthew 25:41).

The second coming of Jesus is a well-known expectation of Christians. It will be an invasion of Earth:

> "Look, he is coming with the clouds," and "every eye will see him, even those who pierced him"; and all peoples on earth "will mourn because of him." (Revelation 1:7 NIV)

> For the Lord himself will come down from heaven, with a loud command, with the voice of the archangel and with the trumpet call of God, and the dead in Christ will rise first. (1 Thessalonians 4:16)

These verses are sung in hymns and are widely known even among those who do not adhere to the Christian faith. What many do not know is that before the coming of Christ the devil will appear to counterfeit Jesus' appearing. The world is already being massaged to accept Satan as Christ. The events unfolding in our world has made the climate right for a savior. Will you accept the Son of God, or fall for the deception and accept Satan instead? "And no marvel; for Satan himself is transformed into an angel of light" (2 Corinthians 11:14).

Revelation 17 outlines these events, and reminds us not to marvel – these things will come to pass.

Let us be ready for the deception and align ourselves with God and his true believers, who have "washed their robes in the blood of the Lamb, who keep his commandments and have the faith of Jesus" (Revelation 7:14; 14:12)

Death

Living on my street is for me an experience. I get to see all ranges of people, from babes in strollers to small children, adolescents, young adults, mature adults to the very old, full of wisdom. There is little difference among the houses, from newly constructed to renovated to historic homes where all the history is preserved. Yet, there is something else that makes this street unique – the funeral home. From the cars lining the road, to the onlookers questioning what might have happened, there is no doubt when a life has been lost.

At times I wonder whether it was an old person, who passed away quietly in their sleep, or someone stricken by one of many diseases, possibly cancer or liver disease. Was it a terrible accident or, worse, was it a child who never got a chance at life? I usually assume it is an old person who has lived a long life, but has now expired. How naive! And considering the average life expectancy in Canada is 81 years, to me that's not even old. Is 16 years post retirement all the average person can expect? This makes me consider the meaning of death – what happens then? Is that it, for those years lived?

Many believe the dead go directly to heaven or hell, with some believing in purgatory – a holding place between heaven and hell. What is the state of the dead? Do they go directly to heaven or hell, can they hear us when we speak, are they over-looking us from heaven, or burning continually in hell?

To figure out the answer I did a little digging in a source I've found trustworthy – the Bible.

It describes two things coming together to make Adam. One was the body, plus the second, the breath; these two combined and made a living soul: "And the LORD God formed man of the dust of the ground, and breathed into his nostrils the breath of life; and man became a living soul" (Genesis 2:7).

Likewise, at death these two are separated – the breath returns to God and the body to the ground:

> Then shall the dust return to the earth as it was: and the spirit shall return unto God who gave it. (Ecclesiastes 12:7)

> And when Jesus had cried with a loud voice, he said, Father, into thy hands I commend my spirit: and having said thus, he gave up the ghost. (Luke 23:46)

> His breath goeth forth, he returneth to his earth; in that very day his thoughts perish. (Psalm 146:4)

What does that mean? To make it as simple as possible, everyone living comprises both a body and spirit/breath, but at death the breath is separated from the body. We can die many ways, the body being destroyed, or the breath being taken by God. This is implied in the text "Fear not them which kill the body, but are not able to kill the soul: but rather fear him which is able to destroy both soul and body in hell" (Matthew 10:28).

Here is the good news, at death the soul is not destroyed, but asleep. Lazarus a dead man by our understanding, was considered asleep: "Our friend Lazarus has fallen asleep; but I am going there to wake him up" (John 11:11 NIV).

Asleep and awaiting the call only God can give. While we may have many caskets passing through our streets, let us not consider them dead but only asleep. And if they are only asleep they will one day wake up again. So, let us be comforted by this, and until the call comes may all those souls "Rest in Peace" and be comforted by this news.

When the call does come it will resemble the following:

> The tombs were opened, and many bodies of the saints who had fallen asleep were raised. (Matthew 27:52 NKJV)

> Many of those who sleep in the dust of the ground will awake, these to everlasting life, but the others to disgrace and everlasting contempt. (Daniel 12:2)

While I have shared the good news, there is more. Those who are asleep will awake, but their destination is already determined by the life they lived:

> Do not marvel at this; for an hour is coming, in which all who are in the tombs will hear His voice, and will come forth; those who did the good deeds to a resurrection of life, those who committed the evil deeds to a resurrection of judgment. (John 5:28–29)

> And I saw the dead, the great and the small, standing before the throne, and books were opened; and another book was opened, which is the book of life; and the dead were judged from the things which were written in the books, according to their deeds. And the sea gave up the dead which were in it, and death and Hades gave up the dead which were in them; and they were judged, every one of them according to their deeds. (Revelation 20:12–13)

Let's consider the life we are living, let us consider the deeds done to our bodies, and let us make a decision to commit only good deeds. As the wise man Solomon once said, "Let us hear the conclusion of the whole matter: Fear God, and keep his commandments: for this *is* the whole *duty* of man" (Ecclesiastes 12:13).

Be comforted, knowing that all those who have passed are resting, awaiting the Lord's wake-up call.

Popular
Holidays

St. Patrick's Day

It is St. Patrick's Day! The story of Patrick is increasingly relevant considering the events that occurred this week as a result of COVID-19.

Kidnapped at the age of 16 by Irish/Celtic pirates from his home, Patrick was forced to work as a slave for six years tending the sheep of Irish King Miliucc. It was during this time in isolation, socially distant from his family and friends, that Patrick used the time to think. While sitting in the fields with the sheep, Patrick thought of the Christian God his father worshipped. Before his kidnapping he considered the Christian God one for fools. Patrick wrote, "The lord opened the shame of my unbelief."

Patrick now found comfort in Jesus during the years in isolation. These years became the ones of his conversion, and ultimately the most important for his spiritual development. The fear and love of God were so fully consumed in his spirit that in a single day or night he would offer over a hundred prayers.

One night during his dream, Patrick heard a voice say, "Patrick your hungers are rewarded; you are going home." "Blessed are those who hunger and thirst for righteousness, for they will be filled" (Matthew 5:6 NIV).

He woke thinking it was only a dream, but the voice continued, "Look your ship is ready." Patrick would return to his family in Britain.

> "In the last days, God says, I will pour out my Spirit on all people. Your sons and daughters will prophesy, your young men will see visions, your old men will dream dreams" (Acts 2:17 NIV).

His family hoped he would stay for the rest of his life; however, it was not meant to be. In another dream he saw an angel holding a batch of letters, with one that had written at the top "Vox Hiberionacum," the "Voice of the Hibernians" (the Irish). Patrick would ignore the dream, but it kept coming, until he heard the voice of Jesus himself: "He who gave his life for you, he it is who speaks within you." At this point, he could no longer ignore the dream, and traveled to Gaul to study for the ministry, and then to Ireland to live among the people who had stolen his youth.

Patrick would share the gospel with the Irish, and they listened and turned to Christianity. King Aengus was baptized by Patrick at the Rock of Cashel. Ireland was transformed by Patrick's ministry: he established centers of Christian learning, the slave trade ended, the wars between Irish chiefs waned, and many learned to read and write. Irish monks lived in simple abbeys, with twelve disciples, and spent their days preaching, teaching, learning and copying the Scriptures. This all occurred against the backdrop of the Dark Ages.

Patrick and his ministry allowed the apostolic Christian faith to thrive, and the Scriptures were preserved, safely secluded from the compromise and corruption occurring in Rome. "Heaven and earth will pass away, but my words will never pass away" (Luke 21:33).

While many of us are self-isolating, now is as good a time as any to consider our faith and the many promises the early Celtic believers took to heart.

Patrick and the early Celtic believers had a profound love for the Bible – it was their ultimate rule of faith. They believed in the power of prayer and that the Creator God heard their prayers. This is shown in how Patrick prayed upward of 100 times a day. They also believed in a literal return of Christ and kept the seventh-day Sabbath.

Wherever you are in faith, these days will be trying, and will be a time of reflection and contemplation. I hope, like Patrick, you find comfort in Jesus: "Come to me, all you who are weary and burdened, and I will give you rest. Take my yoke upon you and learn from me, for I am gentle and humble in heart, and you will find rest for your souls" (Matthew 11:28–29).

Thanksgiving and Halloween

As the end of the year approaches, the celebrations of significant days become more frequent. This month many celebrated Thanksgiving with family and friends. In October we have Remembrance Day and in December we can expect celebration of Christmas and the new year. These days have been celebrated without fail, so much so that we often forget what is being celebrated and why. I had to check to be sure I really understood the significance of thanksgiving for Canadians. To my surprise I learned that Canada was the first country to celebrate Thanksgiving, with the first instance of celebration recorded in 1578. On January 31, 1957, the Governor General of Canada issued a proclamation stating, "A Day of General Thanksgiving to Almighty God for the bountiful harvest with which Canada has been blessed – to be observed on the 2nd Monday in October." In general terms, Thanksgiving is a holiday celebrating the harvest, and the blessing received from God.

There is another celebration in October. While not a holiday, it receives considerable attention, more so than Thanksgiving. Its celebration is second only to Christmas. Halloween will be celebrated by many October 31st, which is a scary thought. But why celebrate Halloween and what is being celebrated? Halloween has its origins in the ancient Celtic festival known as Samhain (pronounced "sah-win"). The ancient Gaels believed that on October 31, the boundaries between the worlds of the living and the dead overlapped and the deceased, along with evil spirits, would come back to life and cause havoc, such as sickness or damaged crops. To avoid such troubles, they would dress up in outfits to disguise themselves as evil spirits. Trick-or-treat, imported into North America by immigrants, involved the poor begging for what were called soul cakes, and in return they would pray for dead relatives, known as "souling." In general terms Halloween is a celebration of death, and being possessed by evil spirits. Quite the opposite of Thanksgiving.

Our society has increasingly become obsessed with death, vampires, zombies, zombie walks and the like. I see skulls on clothing, water bottles, pencils and the simplest things. On Halloween, this obsession climaxes with over 8 billion dollars being spent on merchandise, costumes, and events, while thousands struggle across the world to find food and shelter. Violent crime on Halloween will be up by 50%, according to a study done by the professor of criminology at Northeast University in Boston. Which begs the question, is this all innocent fun, or more sinister than many are led to believe? Recently, there have been some creepy clown issues, "clownpocalypse" as some call it, in Toronto and neighboring cities, which highlights the level of vice prevalent.

This Halloween it is my hope that you will consider the depth of evil that surrounds Halloween. This is the same evil many parents will baptize their children in, with many appearing as monsters, vampires and zombies, some superheroes and princesses, inviting demonic possession rather than warding them off as once thought. Consider the following: "Beloved, follow not that which is evil, but that which is good. He that doeth good is of God: but he that doeth evil hath not seen God" (2 John 1:11).

It is unwise to participate in these types of activities after being armed with knowledge of their history. Consider your motives and review your decision-making if you plan to participate. Keep the following in mind: "Dear friend, do not imitate what is evil but what is good. Anyone who does what is good is from God. Anyone who does what is evil has not seen God" (3 John 1:11).

Lastly, don't be fooled into making the mistake of thinking Halloween is innocent. Rather, be mindful of the conditions surrounding Halloween: "You cannot drink the cup of the Lord and the cup of demons too; you cannot have a part in both the Lord's table and the table of demons" (1 Corinthians 10:21 NIV).

Every day of our life we make many decisions, some small and some large, with varying consequences. Choose to participate in godly activities and "save yourself from this wicked and corrupt generation" (Acts 2:40 NIV).

Choose the light and the life, and have a wonderful day.

Remembrance Day

November 11 marks the anniversary of the end of World War I in 1918. The famous poem written by Canadian physician Lieutenant-Colonel John McCrae, "In Flanders Fields," has resulted in many wearing poppies to recall the sacrifice made by Canadian soldiers during the war. On Remembrance Day, we typically spend a silent minute reflecting on lives lost at war. James Lornier catches the essence of Remembrance Day in this quote:

> We must remember. If we do not, the sacrifice of those one hundred thousand Canadian lives will be meaningless. They died for us, for their homes and families and friends, for a collection of traditions they cherished and a future they believed in; they died for Canada. The meaning of their sacrifice rests with our collective national consciousness; our future is their monument. (Source: https://www.veterans.gc.ca/eng/remembrance/history/a-day-of-remembrance/why)

The sacrifice our ancestors made, has left us heirs of the many freedoms we enjoy today. Unfortunately, it is now apparent with each passing day how we have neglected our responsibility to protect these freedoms, which required the most precious of all costs – human life. With all the conflicts brewing across the world, and in the USA, war is inevitably part of our future.

Notwithstanding, there is another subtler, but equally or more devastating, war, resulting in the most catastrophic consequence of all – death:

> And there was war in heaven: Michael and his angels fought against the dragon; and the dragon fought and his angels, And prevailed not; neither was their place found any more in heaven. And the great dragon was cast out, that old serpent, called the Devil, and Satan, which deceiveth the whole world: he was cast out into the earth, and his angels were cast out with him. And I heard a loud voice saying in heaven, Now is come salvation, and strength, and the kingdom of our God, and the power of his Christ: for the accuser of our brethren is cast down, which accused them before our God day and night. And they overcame him by the blood of the Lamb, and by the word of their testimony; and they loved not their lives unto the death. (Revelation 12:7–11)

The war is between good and evil. In this war, casualties face both physical and spiritual death. Many confuse this war with others fought with a religious nature. As a matter of fact, it is not unusual to hear many people say most wars are fought as a result of religion. While true, it blurs the heart of the matter. The war of which I speak is not a collective war of soldiers but an independent battle for our soul, waged in every heart. It requires loving something more than life itself, similar to those who gave their lives in past wars.

> Put on the full armor of God, so that you can take your stand against the devil's schemes. For our struggle is not against flesh and blood, but against the rulers, against the authorities, against the powers of this dark world and against the spiritual forces of evil in the heavenly realms. Therefore put on the full armor of God, so that when the day of evil comes, you may be able to stand your ground, and after you have done everything, to stand. Stand firm then, with the belt of truth buckled around your waist, with the breastplate of righteousness in place, and with your feet fitted with the readiness that comes from the gospel of peace. In addition to all this, take up the shield of faith, with which you can extinguish all the flaming arrows of the evil one. Take the helmet of salvation and the sword of the Spirit, which is the word of God.

(Ephesians 6:11–17)

An intelligent person would not deny the existence of good and evil, but somehow many are indifferent about God and the devil. There is only one way to overcome evil: "Be not overcome of evil, but overcome evil with good" (Romans 12:21). "Depart from evil, and do good; and dwell for ever more" (Psalm 37:27).

As the cosmic battle between good and evil is waged, each person must select a side. You can be on God's side or the devil's side, the side of good, or evil. Many are fighting a losing battle, many have been held as prisoners of war, captive to various sins; some are weary after years of vigilant fighting. Wherever you find yourself today, I encourage you to keep fighting, as the war is a perpetual war and will not cease until Jesus returns and proclaims it is finished.

> And he said unto me, It is done. I am Alpha and Omega, the beginning and the end. I will give unto him that is athirst of the fountain of the water of life freely. (Revelation 21:6–7 NIV)

Just as we are able to enjoy the freedoms a country such as Canada offers, so too will we be able to enjoy the joys of being victorious over evil, and inherit all the things God has prepared. Choose to fight on God's side, fighting daily to live a fruitful life, experiencing "love, joy, peace, longsuffering, gentleness, goodness, faith, Meekness, temperance" (Galatians 5:22–25).

Lastly, remember, there is only one way to be victorious in battle: "they overcame him by the blood of the Lamb, and by the word of their testimony; and they loved not their lives unto the death." As tough to accept as it may be, war is won only by sacrifice, and the sacrifice of life: "For God so loved the world, that he gave his only begotten son that whosoever believeth in him should not perish but have everlasting life" (John 3:16).

The sacrifice has already been made – all that is missing is the word of our testimony.

Christmas

Over 2000 years ago three wise men greeted the baby Jesus with gifts fit for a king. You may even hear the song sung about them during the holiday period "We three kings of Orient are, bearing gifts we traverse afar." Who are these wise men, how did they know about Jesus' birth, and why were they willing to travel from so far away?

This group of wise men date back to the time of Daniel the prophet. These were the men once sentenced to death for failure to interpret the dream of the King (Daniel 2:13). Daniel prayed and received the interpretation of the dream and spared the wise men's lives. Daniel had a gift from God to understand visions and dreams (Daniel 5:11). Daniel saw the full unraveling of Earth's history. He saw the rise and fall of kingdoms, the birth of Jesus, his baptism, death, and second coming. The prophecies regarding Jesus are found in Daniel chapter 9. This prophecy is referred as the 70-week prophecy. This knowledge was passed down the ages by the wise men long after Daniel died. Now when the signs were fulfilled the wise men recognized them and acted upon them. They set out with gifts to worship the creator of the world.

The wise men brought gold, frankincense, and myrrh, each gift a symbol of an aspect of Jesus' life. Gold represents his kingship. Frankincense was a symbol of him as God. Frankincense is an incense, and historically was used in worship (Psalm 141:2). Lastly, myrrh an embalming oil, was the symbol for his death. These gifts reinforce that these wise men knew the significance of the birth of the baby Jesus:

> Then Herod, when he had privily called the wise men, inquired of them diligently what time the star appeared. And he sent them to Bethlehem, and said, Go and search diligently for the young child; and when ye have found him, bring me word again, that I may come and worship him also. When they had heard the king, they departed; and, lo, the star, which they saw in the east, went before them, till it came and stood over where the young child was. When they saw the star, they rejoiced with exceeding great joy. And when they were come into the house, they saw the young child with Mary his mother, and fell down, and worshipped him: and when they had opened their treasures, they presented unto him gifts; gold, and frankincense, and myrrh. (Matthew 2:7–11 NIV)

Herod, in fear he will be overthrown as ruler, attempts to kill the baby Jesus (Matthew 2:12–13). However, the wise men are warned in a dream not to return to Herod. Nothing can stop the purposes of God (Acts 5:39).

Jesus' first coming was preceded with signs in the sun, moon, and stars. So will be his second coming. However, the signs will be given by the son of God, the light of the world, Jesus Christ (Matthew 24). Are you like the wise men, recognizing these signs, and are you ready with your gifts to worship him?

Let us remember the wise men, who knew the prophecies concerning Jesus' coming and were ready to meet him. I hope you too will be ready to meet him at his second coming.

THE SABBATH

THE FUTURE REST

In the era of climate change, rest for the environment has become a political speaking point. The lockdowns introduced in response to the pandemic produced significant benefits for our world. The water bodies and the air, for example, were cleaner than in the recent past. These results have solidified the benefits rest provides. If our world can benefit from rest, can we not also? This was God's design when he created the Sabbath.

At creation, God created the earth in six days and rested on the seventh day:

> Thus the heavens and the earth were finished, and all the host of them. And on the seventh day God ended his work which he had made; and he rested on the seventh day from all his work which he had made. And God blessed the seventh day, and sanctified it: because that in it he had rested from all his work which God created and made. (Genesis 2:1–3)

This act of creation is why God calls us to worship him:

> Remember the sabbath day, to keep it holy. Six days shalt thou labor, and do all thy work: But the seventh day is the sabbath of the LORD thy God: in it thou shalt not do any work, thou, nor thy son, nor thy daughter, thy manservant, nor thy maidservant, nor thy cattle, nor thy stranger that is within thy gates: For in six days the LORD made heaven and earth, the sea, and all that in them is, and rested the seventh day: wherefore the LORD blessed the sabbath day, and hallowed it. (Exodus 20:8–11)

This command forever fixed the Sabbath day as a day of worship, where we recognize God as the creator of the world. God as Creator is not the only reason why the Sabbath was established as a day of worship. In the second reading of the law, Moses pointed out to the children of Israel that they ought to keep the Sabbath holy because God rescued them from slavery in Egypt:

> Keep the sabbath day to sanctify it, as the LORD thy God hath commanded thee. Six days thou shalt labor, and do all thy work: But the seventh day is the sabbath of the LORD thy God . . . And remember that thou wast a servant in the land of Egypt, and that the LORD thy God brought thee out thence through a

mighty hand and by a stretched out arm: therefore the LORD thy God commanded thee to keep the sabbath day. (Deuteronomy 5:12–15)

The second reason why the Sabbath day was kept was to recognize God as one who delivered the children of Israel from Egypt. Today, believers in Jesus are grafted in as part of the Israel of old (Romans 11). As a result, there remains a sabbath rest for believers in Jesus Christ:

> There remaineth therefore a rest to the people of God. For he that is entered into his rest, he also hath ceased from his own works, as God did from his. Let us labour therefore to enter into that rest, lest any man fall after the same example of unbelief. (Hebrew 4:9–11)

Analogous to the Israel of old we observe the Sabbath for the same two reasons. One, God as the creator of the world. Two, God as the one who takes us out of the bondage of sin.

Could the Israelites have taken themselves out of bondage? Can we break our bondage to sin? No! Our hope is in the promised deliverer Jesus Christ. We rest weekly on the seventh day as commanded, to worship God as the Creator. We also worship him as the Redeemer, the one who has taken us out of the bondage to sin. Worship is not a trivial matter: disobedience provokes the Lord to anger and places his people under judgment (Ezekiel 8:17).

Lastly, we are called to worship on the seventh day looking forward to his millennial rest. A day is like 1,000 years with God (2 Peter 3:8). For 6,000 years our earth has been in existence. During these 6,000 years God has worked to reclaim his creation. On the seventh day, the last millennium, he will put an end to his work:

> And they lived and reigned with Christ for a thousand years But the rest of the dead did not live again until the thousand years were finished. This is the first resurrection. Blessed and holy is he who has part in the first resurrection. Over such the second death has no power, but they shall be priests of God and of Christ and shall reign with Him a thousand years. (Revelation 20:4–7)

Until he comes again, and we get to experience reigning with Christ, let us rest in the completed work of Jesus.

> Fear God and give him glory, because the hour of his judgment has come. Worship him who made the heavens, the earth, the sea and the springs of water. (Revelation 14:7)